Weather Watchers

Wind

Cassie Mayer

www.heinemann.co.uk/library
Visit our website to find out more information about **Heinemann Library** books.

To order:
☎ Phone 44 (0) 1865 888066
🖨 Send a fax to 44 (0) 1865 314091
💻 Visit the Heinemann Bookshop at www.heinemann.co.uk/library to browse our catalogue and order online.

First published in Great Britain by Heinemann Library, Halley Court, Jordan Hill, Oxford OX2 8EJ, part of Harcourt Education. Heinemann is a registered trademark of Harcourt Education Ltd.

Editorial: Tracey Crawford, Cassie Mayer, Dan Nunn, and Sarah Chappelow
Design: Jo Hinton-Malivoire
Picture Research: Tracy Cummins, Tracey Engel, and Ruth Blair
Production: Duncan Gilbert

Originated by Chroma Graphics (Overseas) Pte. Ltd
Printed and bound in China by South China Printing Company

10 digit ISBN 0 431 18260 4
13 digit ISBN 978 0 431 18260 5

11 10 09 08 07
10 9 8 7 6 5 4 3 2 1

British Library Cataloguing in Publication Data
Mayer, Cassie
    Wind. - (Weather watchers)
    1.Winds - Juvenile literature
    I.Title
    551.5'18
A full catalogue record for this book is available from the British Library.

Acknowledgements
The publishers would like to thank the following for permission to reproduce photographs: Alamy p. **15** (Michael Dwyer); Corbis pp. **4** (cloud; rain, Anthony Redpath), **5** (C/B Productions), **7** (George H. H. Huey), **9**, **11** (Lowell Georgia), **13** (China Newsphoto/ Reuters), **14** (Lawrence Manning), **19** (Jim Reed/Jim Reed Photography), **20** (epa/Anatoly Maltsev), **21** (Ariel Skelley), **23** (hurricane, Jim Reed/Jim Reed Photography); Getty pp. **4** (lightning; snow, Marc Wilson Photography), **6** (Bob Elsdale), **8** (The Image Bank/Laurence Dutton), **10** (Panoramic Images), **12** (Asia Images/Mary Grace Long), **16** (National Geographic/Gordon Wiltsie), **18** (A T Willet), **23** (tornado, A T Willet); Shutterstock p. **22** (windsock with wind, Steven Robertson; windsock with no wind, Anders Brownworth; weather vane, Robert Kyllo; windmill, Barry Hurt).

Cover photograph reproduced with permission of Corbis (Royalty Free). Back cover photograph reproduced with permission of Reuters (China Newsphoto).

Every effort has been made to contact copyright holders of any material reproduced in this book. Any omissions will be rectified in subsequent printings if notice is given to

Contents

What is weather?

There are many types of weather.
Weather changes all the time.

A windy day is a type of weather.
Wind is blowing these flags.

What is wind?

Wind is moving air.

Wind moves in many directions.

You can feel wind.

You cannot see wind but
you can see what it does.

Wind blows across land.

Wind blows across water.

Wind can be gentle.

Wind can be strong.

What does wind do?

Wind can blow warm air.

Wind can blow cold air.

Types of wind

Some winds blow in different directions all the time.

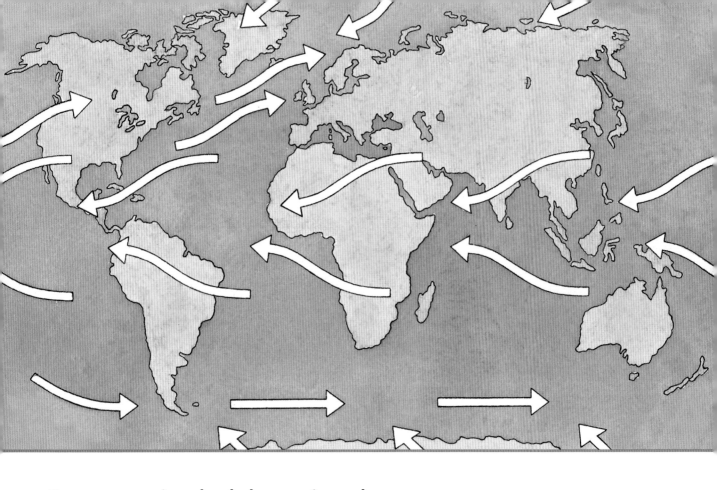

Some winds blow in the same
direction for a long time.

Dangerous winds

A tornado is a type of wind
that spins very fast.

A hurricane is a type of wind
that is very powerful.

How does wind help us?

Wind can bring rain.

Wind can bring a sunny day.
Windy days can be fun!

Wind tools

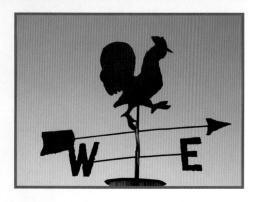

This is a weather vane. It shows which direction the wind is blowing in.

These are wind turbines. They use the wind to make electricity.

This is a wind sock. It shows which direction the wind is blowing in. It also shows how hard the wind is blowing.

Picture glossary

hurricane a big storm with strong winds

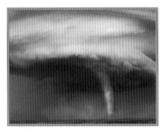

tornado a tower of air that spins very fast

Index

Notes to parents and teachers
Before reading
Talk about different weather. Ask the children which type of weather they like best. Have they ever been out on a windy day? What did it feel like?

After reading
Go outside and look around for any evidence of the wind. Can they see the leaves moving on a tree or on the ground? Can they feel the wind on their faces?
Find out the direction of the wind. Tell them to lick a finger and hold it up. Can they feel which way the wind is blowing? Give each child a strip of tissue paper. Tell them to hold it up and see how it blows in the wind.
Play "Flap the fish". Make "flappers" by folding newspaper. Make simple fish shapes out of tissue paper. Challenge the children to race their fish across the hall by flapping the newspaper to create a wind.
Do the actions to the rhyme: Like a leaf or a feather, In the windy, windy weather, Whirl around, and twirl around, And all fall down together.

Titles in the *Weather Watchers* series include:

Hardback 0 431 18258 2

Hardback 0 431 18256 6

Hardback 0 431 18257 4

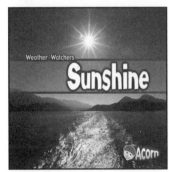

Hardback 0 431 18259 0

Hardback 0 431 18255 8

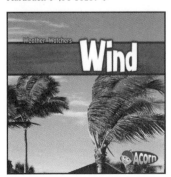

Hardback 0 431 18260 4

Find out about other titles from Heinemann Library on our website www.heinemann.co.uk/library